United We Stand

D1556723

UNITED WE STAND

An illustrated account of
Trade Union Emblems

R. A. LEESON

ADAMS & DART · BATH

Many of the emblems featured in this book have been preserved in the Library of the Trades Union Congress, for whose assistance and co-operation the author and publishers are grateful.

First published in 1971 by
Adams & Dart, 40 Gay Street, Bath, Somerset
SBN 239 00089 7
Printed in Great Britain by Butler & Tanner Ltd

List of Illustrations

United We Stand

Trade unions are a British invention, one of the most important of the Industrial Revolution and one that still vitally affects life today, while most other products of that time belong in museums. Unions grow more powerful, organising, today, nearly one in two employed people in Britain. They do so because, whatever their external critics say, they change. Some of the history of that change is in this book, told through the imaginations of the men who made it.

These nineteenth-century emblems represent the movement as trade unionists saw it themselves and wanted others to see it. Their origins lie well back beyond the 1800s, but their heyday was between 1870 and 1900, when some 100,000 emblems were sold; when in some unions one in three members displayed one on the wall at home; and in hundreds of pubs, as union leader F. W. Galton told Beatrice and Sidney Webb, the walls of upper rooms were decorated with trade society emblems 'interspersed with gold mirrors and advertising almanacs'.

When emblems flourished there were some 1,300 unions in Britain. Of these nearly 1,000 have gone, died out or merged into those that remain. In many cases the emblem—folded into a file, dumped in a loft, or, in one case, backing the lino—is the only trace of what has gone. Of the unions represented here, only three remain in independent existence. Many inheritor unions treasure these glimpses of their past, others are ignorant of them. Yet for anyone, in or out of the unions, who wants to know why unions are as they are, here are valuable and entertaining clues.

Two conflicting views of the trade-union movement strove for ascendancy in the nineteenth century: one the defensive-restrictive gild-craft tradition passed down through journeymen's clubs and friendly societies, the experience-instinct of skilled workers expressed in their mottoes 'united to protect' and to 'keep our rights inviolate'; the other the aggressive-expansionist drive to unite all 'labouring men and women' for a 'different order of things', in the words of the short-lived Grand National Consolidated Trades Union of 1834; an idea appealing to visionary craft workers and now and again to the unskilled with no rights to keep inviolate. This clash between different notions of unity, a clash now sterile, now fruitful, brought both change and compromise, epitomised in the Trades Union Congress and its creation, the Labour Party. And in the clash, with its recurring theme of 'United We Stand', the emblems played their part, sometimes as the signs of the competition between unions, sometimes as the outward appeal, the 'spice advertisement' as one union leader called it.

Emblems begin though, and take their shape, in the first original notion of unity of the craft unions, which the Webbs called the 'jealously democratic state within our state'. This is not a bad description for what were in effect autonomous republics with their own employment, population and emigration policies and apparatus; their welfare system from orphan allowance to funeral

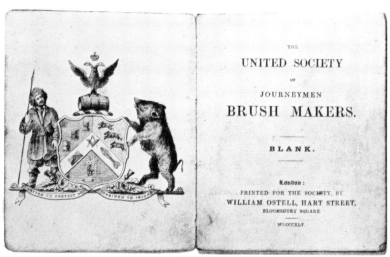

Blank Book of the United Society of Journeymen Brush Makers 1845

benefit; their inner democracy, far more intricate and alive than the official democracy of Parliament which excluded them; their own financial system, laws and customs, check points and passports. The first emblems in fact were the passport stamp on the 'blank book' which eighteenth-century trade clubs and sometimes Friendly Societies gave their members when 'bad trade' times, victimisation or simply wanderlust—'let me put my foot on daisies'—drove them to tramp the roads searching work.

William Kiddier, in his *The Old Trade Unions*, says that 'The Society of Brushmakers was formed in the process of linking up the towns by a system of tramping. In those days each society of importance provided members with an engraving of the Brushmakers arms. As local societies, each had a different design and different motto and date of foundation, but all showed the Russian wild boar, the authentic sign of the trade'.

With his blank book authentically stamped and contributions paid the tramp was entitled in each town where his society had a 'house of call' to a night's bed, supper and a social pint of beer, perhaps in a mug bearing the society's emblem in transfer. So the blank book was a record of his journeyings.

When the United Society of Brushmakers was formed by a 'mutual understanding between a number of towns' a suitable emblem was issued. This rare example, designed and engraved by J. Shury of Charterhouse Lane, London, cost 'about 6d' a copy on India paper. By the time it was completed at the end of 1839, secretary William Hunt had to tell members to be patient, reminding them that 'there is no reliance on the word or promise of an engraver respecting the time he will require to execute a plate like ours'. It embodies the arms of six major towns, the Russian boar, and a view of St Katherine's dock, presumably the import point for bristle cargoes.

For most early unions, those of plasterers, painters, masons, carpenters and joiners, compositors, bricklayers, tinplate workers, shipwrights, weavers, cordwainers, the 'authentic sign of the trade' was the gild coat of arms, often centuries old, complete with religious motto in Latin, though the religious sentiments were being replaced with secular ones, a process already started in the gilds during the Reformation.

With a new post-gild trade, the basic emblem, like that chosen in 1809 by the iron-moulders, was a craft coat of arms in heraldic

United Society of Brushmakers
J. Shury, 1839

style. Even those later unions whose emblems show little trace of heraldic convention, often put out a printed explanation like the blazon of a coat of arms. Thus they followed the medieval tradition that an emblem must contain 'some witty deuice . . . something obscure . . . whereby when with further consideration it is understood, it maie the greater delight the beholder'. In some versions of the ironmoulder's emblem, the two hazy figures in the

Friendly Society of Iron Moulders, mid-nineteenth century

background are shown in conversation:

'Brother craft, can you give me a job?'
'If we cannot, we will assist you.'

The assumption in the question is a very old one based on the tradition that the craft controls the trade, above all who shall enter it. These protective aspects of gild-craft organisation were preserved as far as possible by the journeymen's clubs when the old craft masters in the eighteenth century had abandoned the attempt to regulate the trade, and many of them were following the new factory masters in trying to sweep away controls. It is true that the first acts to ban 'combinations' of workmen were passed by the Pitt Government in 1799 in an atmosphere of anti-

Jacobin hysteria. It is also true that during the 26 years that the Combination Acts operated and the workers' protective organisations were severely hampered, new machinery and processes were introduced on a large scale in mining, engineering, textiles, pottery and other industries, while laws regulating apprenticeship and wage levels were abolished.

The worker had to contend not only with sabre-wielding farmers' sons playing Sunday soldier, but with the most advanced minds of the time, like Wedgwood the potter, preparing to 'make such machines of the men as cannot err', and Nasmyth the engineer, who admired machines because they stayed sober. Small wonder then that craft workers looked back to real or imagined security as well as forward into a promising but problematic future.

The line, or artery through which old ideas flowed into the new age, lay not only in the trade clubs but also in the Friendly Societies. A study of their rules also shows a whole network of surviving, adapted gild regulations, on how to dispense charity, maintain conviviality and regulate behaviour. The Friendly Societies, whose members outnumbered those of the trade clubs by as many as ten to one, were directly and indirectly a reservoir of finance in time of trouble, whether distress was caused by act of God or man, and sometimes sheltered trade activity from prying eyes.

In his splendid work on the Friendly Societies Dr Gosden shows how the Establishment suspected these societies of being merely a cover for feasting or striking—it was not sure which was worse. Friendly Society emblems, like union emblems, show the whole range of medieval craft mystification spiced with freemasonic elaborations from the eighteenth century. The Oddfellows' emblem (a much later version of one issued in the 1820s) is a good example (p. 12).

Many Oddfellows were building craftsmen, heirs to the most ancient traditions. The symbols of unity (the lath bundle), of life (the spindle), of labour (the beehive), of knowledge (the keys), are from the stock of 'historical', 'natural' and 'moral' elements

AMICITIA AMOR ET VERITAS

TO THE
GRAND MASTER, THE BOARD OF DIRECTORS,
and the Order in general.

This is to Certify, That our well beloved
was admitted a Member of the Loyal   July 1st
in the   District of the Independent Order of Odd Fellows
Manchester Unity Friendly Society on the   day of   in the Year
of our Lord One Thousand Nine Hundred and

N G   V G   Secy

which the Elizabethan collector Geoffrey Whitney thought every emblem should have. Chief of all these was the ancient all-seeing eye of the supreme Deity: known to the gilds, expressed cabalistically for alchemists and Rosicrucians as a 'blind point' in a circle, it was one of those craft notions which freemasons elaborated when they invaded the mysteries of 'operative masons' in the seventeenth and eighteenth centuries.

For Oddfellows, so Gosden reports, the all-seeing eye meant for all officers and brothers that 'an unerring providence attends all their ways, pries into their secrets, records all their thoughts and actions'. For the union and Friendly Societies of the 'forties and 'fifties, as they strove to stabilise membership, protect funds and inhibit 'rash action' by independent local groups, the all-seeing eye is that of the central executive, aided by Mr Stephenson's new railway and Mr Hill's new penny post. More seriously, as Galton told the Webbs, the society emblem then became for the member a 'connecting link with the other men in his trade and society' and for his wife 'their charter of rights in sickness and death'.

Arms of the Worshipful Company of Tin-Plate Workers alias Wire Workers 1670

The four emblems of the Tin-Plate workers on the following pages show well the progress of the emblem from travelling coat of arms to certificate on the wall, together with the parallel technical development from copper engraving to chromolithographic, power-driven flat-bed production.

(left) Independent Order of Oddfellows, Manchester Unity

13

This is to certify that Mr.
is a free Member of this Society
and is entitled to receive the Benefits
Stated in the Schedule

Sec.y

N°. Dated this Day of 18
This Card is renewable in four
Months from the Date hereof

(above) Wolverhampton Society of
Tin-Plate Workers 1802

(right) General Union of Tin-Plate Workers
Thomas Duncalf, *c.* 1870

The arms of the Worshipful company of Tin-plate Workers *alias* Wire Workers, 1670, is followed on page 14 by the 1802 emblem of the Wolverhampton Tin-Plate Workers union, while on page 15 is the emblem of the General Union of Tin-Plate Workers launched, mainly by Lancashire clubs, in 1861—a production of the 1870s designed by Thomas Duncalf 'calligrapher to the Queen'. Finally, on page 17, is the lithographed emblem of the National Amalgamated Tin-Plate Workers, launched in 1890 mainly by groups from the Midlands. The 1870s General Union emblem still contains the gild coat of arms, the 1890 emblem does not. The place of the coat of arms has been taken by a mysterious lady. (See page 49).

Some fine emblems come from the time of the great 'Amalgamated' Unions of the 'fifties and 'sixties, with their mixture of craft pride, their old traditions, their trade details in which the artists were carefully drilled, as the account of the mason's emblem later shows. But a transformation is on the way as the unions in those industries most shaped by new conditions—transport, mining, textiles—come into the picture. Craft pride blends with industrial confidence. This is also the period in which the state within the state demands *de jure* recognition in trade union legislation. And the boom in emblems that this caused went step by step with the print changeover from engraving to lithographic mass production, to photo-transfer and printing in colour, instead of applying the tint afterwards.

Bigger changes were to follow, as the new general unions burst on the scene in the late 1880s and 1890s. Here for the moment the advertising of friendly benefits is eclipsed by a confident demand for change, with a list of all the workers the new unions intend to sweep into their net. The slogan replaces the motto, the day-to-day demand replaces the generalised sentiment. In this final stage the emblem flourishes. The union movement is growing from one million to two million members within a decade, with craft and general unions competing in industries that had been static, the emblem becoming part of a publicity drive, with workers in one union asking their leadership if they too can have a specially-

National Amalgamated Tin-Plate Workers c. 1892

OMNIA VINCIT LABOR

The Labourer is worthy of his hire

Our want supplies Labour like this

NATIONAL AMALGAMATED TIN PLATE WORKERS OF GREAT BRITAIN

This is to Certify that _____ was admitted a Member of the _____ Branch of the above Amalgamation on the _____ day of _____

Branch Secretary   General Secretary

designed mark of membership. In the case of the patternmakers the argument went on for 20 years before the leadership gave in. In the miners' emblems appear the portraits of leaders with their newly acquired political titles, the first fruits of the franchise being extended to workers in town and village.

The first emblems are often the creation of worker-artists, like Hughes of the boilermakers. Later, professionals like Chant, Greatbach, Saddler, Waudby and Walter Crane were called in, though none of their work excels the engineers' emblem designed by blacksmith-artist James Sharples. The amalgamated unions paid highly for their emblems, regarding the plates as 'heirlooms'. For a mid-Victorian worker to pay 3s a copy plus 7s for a frame was quite something, but thousands did. In 1857, the iron-founders' secretary is reported to have threatened to resign if he did not get a commission on emblem sales.

Commercial lithography of the last 20 years of the century brought more quickly-produced and colourful emblems with no increase in price, though they began to resemble other products of the big lithographic machine—box labels and posters.

There is the difference, of course, that one is an ephemeral product of advertising, the other, whether expressed with artistic insight or more garishly and crudely, is a part of a remarkable story, part of a century of working-class history.

During the winter evenings of 1834, William Hughes worked on a task entrusted to him by the 14 men who had founded the 'Order of Friendly Boilermakers' in Manchester that summer. He was to work out an opening ceremony and lectures for the benefit of new members and an 'emblematic design by which the society should be easily recognised', an old craft preoccupation. But in designing his emblem Hughes could not simply take a gild coat of arms, for his craft took shape with the age of steam and grew with the railways, bridges and ships with which the Stephensons and the younger Brunel were pushing ahead at that time. But, if there was no gild emblem, there was craft skill and pride in plenty. Hughes and his 13 brothers were launching what was to be one of the most powerful craft unions—still in lively existence today.

Twenty years later Robert Stephenson was to pay a three-guinea honorary membership fee before driving the last rivet on the Menai Bridge. And Hughes had plenty of models for his work, gild emblems like those of the shipwrights or weavers, adapted by local unions. But he was clearly most impressed by the coat of arms of the Friendly United Mechanics, with its locomotive, sail and steam-ship, sun, moon and stars and 'all-seeing eye'. When the emblem was in use as the centre of a membership certificate for the first lodge (a mason's term), meeting at Happy Jack's pub in Bolton, more modifications were added from the iron-moulders' and Oddfellows' emblems.

But to the original emblem Hughes added a boilermaker's recognition sign, the 'uplifting of the hand', and placed it above an

Order of Friendly Boilermakers
1834

heraldic wreath at the emblem's crown. It looks like a direct copy of the centuries-old plasterer's gild emblem, and indeed, in his preamble to the book of rules, the old plasterer's motto is included, 'Let Brotherly Love Continue'. And along with the rule-book, Hughes included not only a hymn and prayer for lodge meetings, provision for lodge drink allowance and drink steward, but also an oath of allegiance not to betray society secrets.

In doing this Hughes was bold. Earlier that year, when the short-lived but splendid recruiting drive of the Grand National Consolidated Trade Union had brought in thousands of members, skilled and unskilled, from masons to chimney sweeps, the

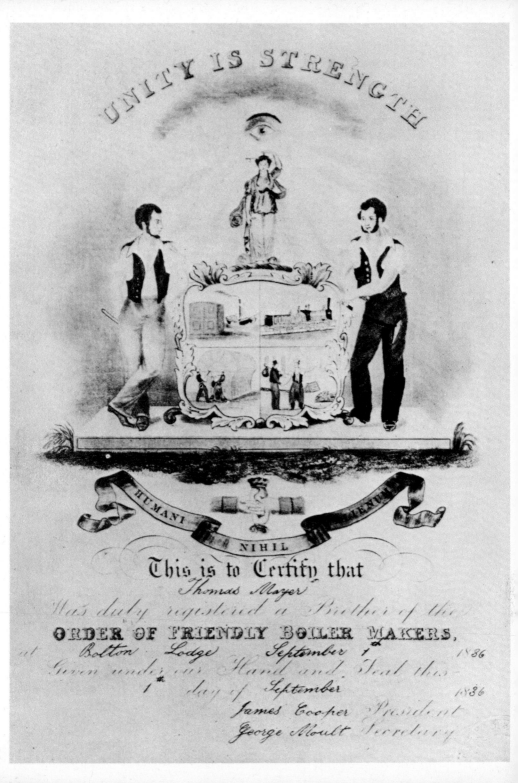

UNITY IS STRENGTH

HUMANI NIHIL ENULI

This is to Certify that
Thomas Mayer
Was duly registered a Brother of the
ORDER OF FRIENDLY BOILER MAKERS,
at Bolton Lodge September 1st 1836
Given under our Hand and Seal this
1st day of September 1836
James Cooper President
George Moult Secretary

Government counter-attacked by martyring the respectable Wesleyan farmworkers from Tolpuddle for 'illegal' oath-taking. Some Lancashire trade clubs and Friendly Societies discontinued their oaths and sold their 'regaler'. But not the boilermakers, for whom the oath must have been as much craft pride as fear of police spies, rooted further back than the Combination Acts of 1799-1800.

Seventy years later D. C. Cummings, in his *Historical Survey of the Boilermakers Society* proudly quoted Hughes' rules at length. Hughes, like most earlier union men, was a 'sincere Christian' and critical of those 'too fond of the carousals of convivial parties', but he still provided for the beer allowance of old trade and friendly club convention. He was no bigot and as the new society's chief motto he chose 'Humani Nihil Alienum', a version of Terence's 'nothing human is indifferent to me'.

Sixteen years after the founding of the Boilermakers' Society, they were invited with ironfounders, engine-makers, mechanics, millwrights and machinists to form the first big 'amalgamation', the Amalgamated Society of Engineers. But the boilermakers, like the United Machine Workers (see page 38) preferred independence. There were, though, two boilermakers' branches which voted for a merger—Swindon and Bury. There must have been friendly relations between boilermakers and engineers in Bury. In the year William Hughes sketched his emblem, James Sharples, artist and life-long ASE member, began work at the age of ten at the Phoenix Factory in Bury. One of 13 children of a Yorkshire ironfounder Sharples, barely able to read and write (his mother had to read his first art manual to him), learnt his draughtsmanship by drawing boiler designs in chalk on the furnace floor, under the direction of the foreman boilermaker.

As he later told Samuel Smiles, Sharples deliberately chose heavier work in the foundry because the heavier jobs took longer to heat, giving him more time for sketching. At 24 he began his most famous work, 'The Forge', and characteristically struggled alone to learn steel engraving in order to produce prints. 'The Forge' took him ten years, was praised by the art journals and sold

Order of Friendly Boilermakers
1836

(above) *Amalgamated Society of Engineers*
James Sharples, 1852

(right) *Friendly Society of Iron Founders*
designed and engraved by
Chant and Saddler, 1857

THE FRIENDLY SOCIETY OF IRON FOUNDERS OF ENGLAND, IRELAND AND WALES,

ESTABLISH'D FEBRUARY 6TH 1809. AT BOLTON LE MOORS, LANCASHIRE.

in thousands. But while he was still at work on it, the new engineers' union (1851) ran a competition for an emblem. 'I determined to compete and I was so fortunate as to win the prize', he wrote to Smiles.

Sharples designed the emblem (page 22), engraved by George Greatbach, a professional on the Victorian equivalent of magazine work, and it was issued, hand-coloured, to members in 1852. Not until the late 'seventies and 'eighties do we find emblems actually printed in colour. The ASE emblem has all the industrial pride of a skilled worker in the year of the Great Exhibition. The traditional parable of the sticks is there, to indicate unity, but the engineer refuses to repair the sword of Mars and a dove of peace replaces the all-seeing eye. The element in trade-union thought that led dozens of unions to affiliate to the first International in the following decade is clearly present.

Sharples was rooked by the art dealers and never got the full reward for 'The Forge'. But the union did not treat him much better. They awarded him £5 for the emblem, and fifty years later a writer in the union Jubilee Souvenir remarked wryly 'He was not overpaid'. But a tight hand on the cash box and tighter control of the independent local bodies were characteristic of William Allan, the new union Secretary. Allan's recipe for stability was widely copied and the ASE emblem must have stimulated the Friendly Society of Iron Founders (the old iron moulders) when they changed their name and rules in the 1850s. They chose to have their emblem produced by professionals (page 23).

James John Chant, engraver and mezzotinter and later exhibitor for over 22 years at the Royal Academy, designed it, and it was engraved by John Saddler, a line engraver who transferred work by Turner, Landseer and Millais to plate. Saddler was well known as a book illustrator and occasionally exhibited at the Royal Academy. The Chant-Saddler emblem is, together with Sharples', one of the finest of the century. The old symbols of labour, immortality, wisdom and unity, the classically draped figures of Art, Commerce and Truth, the figures of the greensand and loam moulders as 'supporters' are in craft tradition, but the central figure of the iron-ore miner imparting unity and drama to the whole is a rare example of artists' license. The assembling of the various obligatory elements and the satisfying of the customers' demand (customers in the plural because branches scrutinised emblem designs before acceptance) could only with difficulty be achieved artistically—and the Chant-Saddler work is such an achievement.

'. . . the interior of a joiner's workshop, all the incidents of which have been carefully drawn on the spot from actual fact with almost photographic exactness' is but one feature admired by the Amalgamated Society of Carpenters in their emblem, which appeared in 1868. India proof copies were supplied at 3s each and plate paper copies at 2s 6d, and thousands were sold to the members of a fast-growing organisation founded in 1860.

It was not the oldest carpenters' union, for the General Union was founded in 1827, an old-style grouping of independent carpenters' branches, with small central funds, ready to fight on trade questions and not interested in friendly benefits. Faced with the challenge of the new 'Amalgamated' which had adopted the rules of the engineers, the General Union tried, almost too late, to provide friendly benefits and strong central funds, and to help increase membership, produced an emblem in 1865, after a competition advertised in several towns. The emblem on page 26 is the reply of the Amalgamated Carpenters, with a fine Renaissance air about it, with Joseph of Nazareth 'most distinguished member of the craft and reputed father of the saviour' riding above an almost exact replica of the joiners' gild coat of arms, though not its motto: the carpenters preferred 'Believe but beware' to 'Join Truth with Trust'. The design of the centring process is taken from the cover of Nicolson's *Practical Carpentry* and the emigration panel at the bottom, one might imagine, was after Ford Madox Brown's 'The Last of England'. In theory emigration would be assisted by the ASCJ when both funds and unemployment were at a high level. As Chandler, General Secretary at a later date, pointed out sardonically, these stipulations made sure no one got an emigration grant easily.

AMALGAMATED SOCIETY OF
CARPENTERS AND JOINERS

The whole was 'engraved on steel in a superior style and no pains spared to make it a work of art satisfactory to the members of the Society as a trade emblem as well as creditable to the artist'. The artist was A. J. Waudby, an exhibitor at the Royal Academy in the 'forties, and for emblems like this he was paid twelve times as much as Sharples got for his. Indeed Waudby must have done very well during the 'sixties, for his success with the carpenters brought him work from the masons, bricklayers and the machinists.

The masons were an old union (1831), a strong force in the builders' parliament which launched the Owenite Gild Hall attempt at worker-run industry in 1833. Preserving the traditions of the old 'operative masons', they were certainly one of the channels through which colourful rites, ceremonies and regalia reached other unions. Their emblem embodies the correct and most ancient masonic gild arms, not the false arms which have been known to fool freemason historians.

Though Richard Harnott, the mason's Secretary, was a tough individual, central control was moderated in his society by older-style democracy. Each issue of importance was debated by the branches and their votes recorded in the Fortnightly Returns, now preserved by the Amalgamated Union of Building Trade Workers, one of the richest sources of union history. The masons in their lodges were, in fact, in permanent session, and it took several months of debate after the Tamworth lodge proposed a new emblem in December 1866 before an 'eminent artist' could be commissioned in August 1867. There was then a 'considerable amount of extra communication in submitting to the artist the usages of the trade in various departments, tools used and the form of attitude of figures when working'.

But when the design was ready a fresh debate broke out. Ware lodge wanted a widow and orphan inserted and the mason's pick removed, because 'masons of the present day have a great dislike for swinging a pick'. Liverpool wanted a mason's trowel inserted. But the Hulme lodge wanted to reject the whole centre panel—the building of the Temple adapted from Raphael's Vati-

Amalgamated Society of Carpenters and Joiners
A. J. Waudby, 1866

can frescoes. 'It is not according to scriptural writ. We read there was not the sound of a hammer or axe nor any tool of iron head in the house while it was building and according to some authors the stone was prepared at the quarries and fitted together and then it was taken to the temple and fixed.' Liverpool and Ware were voted their widow and trowel, but Hulme's doctrinal thesis was rejected, though they were to return to the attack on another front, later. The emblem, which cost £473, was distributed at 2s 9d (frames at 5s and 7s) though only after a long debate about price. The official description throws interesting light on the attitudes of mid-Victorian union leaders. It shows prudence with her bridle 'restraining profuse and needless expenditure' and temperance with 'her ewers of water', not to forget the all-seeing eye. And like an increasing number of emblems it included leaders' portraits: Harnott himself and the president, Thomas Connolly, a flamboyant character who had caused a stir at the hearings of the Royal Commission on the Trade Unions. This was to lead to trouble. The first 3,000 emblems were sold rapidly but 'bad trade' held up production of more during 1870 and 1871.

Early in 1872, when lodges were once more invited to send in orders, the Hulme branch struck again, demanding that emblem orders be suspended. The reason was that one of the figures on the emblem was dead and the other was no longer a member. This was true: Harnott had died in February and Connolly, who had been in America, had lapsed membership. This was unforgivable, and news came that some lodges had covered his figure on the emblem with blank paper. This figure, said London North lodge, was adorning 'the wall of every mason's house much against the wish of many'. Some lodges went further and demanded that both Harnott and Connolly be removed. Let it be a 'real trade emblem and not a photograph of any particular man's popularity' said Southwark. But Connolly and particularly Harnott had their defenders. Many lodges argued that to remove Harnott would be an insult to his memory. Lancashire branches waxed sarcastic, Bolton asking 'are we to be cutting and mangling the plate every time a brother happens to run out?'

Stone Masons' Friendly Society
A. J. Waudby, 1868

Practical considerations and the diplomatic announcement by acting General Secretary J. E. Dyer that Connolly had reappeared and was once more a fully-paid-up member, swayed the vote, which was 737 to 235 against alteration. It was one of the higher votes of the time and the dispute was undoubtedly linked with the election for a new general secretary, which eventually Dyer won. Soon the emblem was selling briskly again and some 5,000 were sold, one for every three members.

Waudby designed emblems not only for unions but for the very successful new central Friendly Societies, which had gone through the same process of amalgamation, concentration, strengthening and becoming more businesslike, while dispensing with the older, less careful, more convivial, 'celebrate and share out', habits of the local societies.

Founded in 1841, the Hearts of Oak Society was the first of the Friendlies with no social functions, dealing strictly in insurance and savings. This Waudby acquatint shows well the new trend. The tradition here is the official one, with the navy's wooden walls representing security, rather than the craft-heraldic notions of Oddfellows', Druids' and Foresters' emblems. As the centralised Friendly Societies frowned on money spent on beer at club nights (the 'wet rent'), so the centralised unions grew increasingly critical of 'rash strikes', of men who in the words of the carpenters' leaders 'waked to the power of organisation, paid their first contribution and forthwith demanded a fight'.

Watching over both forms of backsliding was the all-seeing eye of the Chief Registrar of Friendly Societies, to whom the engineers, carpenters and boilermakers went to seek protection for their funds under the 1855 Act—designed to guard Friendly Societies from embezzlement. In 1867 the boilermakers tried to sue their Bradford secretary, and learned to their dismay that they were still outside the law. The campaign which they and the other major unions launched to remedy this was a major factor leading to the setting up of the Trades Union Congress and the Trade Union Acts of 1871-75. But when the TUC met, at the invitation of the Manchester and Salford Trades Council, in Whit

Hearts of Oak Society
A. J. Waudby, *c.* 1869

Week, 1868, one of its architects, trades-council chairman Nicolson, was not there. He found it, so A. E. Musson reports in *The Congress of 1868*, more suitable to attend the Annual Moveable Delegation of the Order of Druids, of which he was a leader. Having to make the choice between the embryonic TUC and the 50,000 strong Druids Friendly Society (33,000 in Lancashire) he chose the older organisation.

Boilermakers celebrated their new-found legality and respectability after the Trade Union Acts and the mid-seventies boom prosperity with a new emblem. Its atmosphere is industrial rather than craft, with a strong emphasis on friendly benefits. The panel of the Saltash Bridge, based perhaps on Thomas Valentine Robins' oil painting of the Royal opening in 1859, emphasises the link with bridge-builders which strengthened the society. Thirty years later Cummings thought the emblem with technical adaptations would last another thirty. He felt too that it preserved the spirit of Hughes' original emblem (page 19).

But Hughes' motto 'Humani Nihil Alienum' was replaced by 'God helps those who help themselves'.

The 1870s opened with an enormous rush of union organising among textile workers, miners, builders' labourers, patternmakers, railway men and farmworkers, spreading well out beyond the tight craft union circle and foreshadowing the general union explosion of 20 years later.

1872 saw the launching of the Amalgamated Society of Railway Servants, of Joseph Arch's agricultural workers union and the Amalgamated Association of Miners, bringing in a quarter of a million workers, many of whom had little previous experience of union organisation. The patternmakers of the North-East, who that year emerged from their fight for the nine-hour day to start their own union, declining to join the ASE, were mainly non-unionists and very inexperienced.

Fifty years later, William Mosses recorded in his history of the patternmakers (of which he was the General Secretary) how after a few months the Newcastle branch voted to break up and

United Society of Boilermakers
Late 1870s

(above) Amalgamated Society of
Operative Cotton Spinners 1882

(right) Amalgamated Society of
Lithographic Printers 1889

SENEFELDER

LEVER PRESS 1796

STAR PRESS 1806

TOP LEVER PRESS 1820

CYLINDER PRESS 1840

This is to Certify that
was admitted a Member of the Branch of
THE AMALGAMATED SOCIETY
OF
LITHOGRAPHIC PRINTERS
of Great Britain & Ireland,
on the day of 18
Geo B Kelley
GENERAL SECRETARY

LATEST 1888

share out, in old Friendly Society style, rushing down from the branch room into the bar to celebrate. But the Chairman, putting his back to the door, voted the branch back into life.

Cotton spinners, aristocrats of the industry, fighters for nearly a hundred years and backbone of Doherty's famous National Association for the Protection of Labour in 1829, reshaped their organisation at least three times before 1870, when they finally established the Amalgamated Society of Operative Cotton Spinners. Their emblem (page 34), dating from 1882, the work of the firm of Gow, Butterfield, reflects strong industrial pride, the only benefits interesting them being the well known ones of 'out of work' and accident.

They ordered 3,000 emblems selling at 3s each to the members, and if all were sold, then the proportion was high, for only later did they achieve their high level of organisation. There is a Lancashire touch about the motto 'Justice is all we require, we expect nothing less'. James Mawdsley, who signed it, was a Tory candidate, running partner at Oldham in 1899 with Winston Churchill, apparently with members' blessing, it being the spinners' canny decision to seek political justice from whatever party could be compelled to yield it.

The growing textile industry boosted the printing trade, particularly its lithographic section, which took over the printing of patterns and labels from the old copper-plate and wood-block processes. Technical progress was swift and inevitably had its effect, beneficial and otherwise, on the art side with the application of power, the use of photography to transfer images to the lithographic stone, and printing directly in colour, instead of dusting on colour afterwards (thirsty work which provided a good excuse for beer allowance in early litho-printers' branches).

In this period, 1870-1900, when Joseph Pennell declared that commerce drove out art, trade periodicals like the *British Printer* and *British Lithographer* were filled with increasingly lavish supplements in colour and increasingly boastful claims by printers. In December 1890, master-printer Alf Cook of Leeds. advertised in the *Lithographer* a sample colour print produced at

'1260 copies an hour'. His claim was indignantly repudiated by George Kelley, writing from Manchester, who declared that the machine had in fact only been run at less than half that speed.

Kelley had other reasons for being angry with Cook, for he was General Secretary of the Amalgamated Society of Lithographic Printers, formed in 1880 mainly by groups in the North, and Cook at the head of the Yorkshire Printers was trying to squeeze the life out of the new society, after a sharp clash over the 54-hour week. Unsuccessfully, however, for in nine years the Litho-printers, with 2,000 members and £2,000 in the bank, were celebrating with their new emblem (page 35), with its coat-of-arms centrepiece designed by German lithographers and its pictorial history of the industry, from Senefelder's first stone in 1798 to the 'latest' power-driven press on which the emblem itself was printed.

The motto 'The Stones Speak' is a traditional heraldic play on words, as are the letters ENS in the coat of arms. Together with the German word for 'fields' they make up in heraldic rebus style the name of the great founder who looks benevolently down.

When the emblem was produced by Blades, East and Blades in 1889 the members were reassured that both the foreman and machine hand, as society members, would stake their reputation on the quality of the job. The women on the machines shown in the emblem are a special lithographic feature, and it was not unknown for a machine-hand to marry his 'layer-on'.

An added guarantee of the quality of the emblem was the supervision of Mr Rowland Blades, son of the printer. Rowland's father William, patriarch of the firm, pillar of the city, one time Lord Mayor, print scholar and expert on Caxton, had another sort of reputation. As the *British Printer* said in December 1890, his views 'in favour of trade unionism are pretty well known'. So well did he speak out at the London School Board and other institutions against giving work to printing houses which did not offer fair pay and conditions that the London Compositors in 1889 voted him an illuminated address, which Rowland produced on the firm's press 'without the knowledge of the recipient'. In reply the old man urged the union members to fresh missionary

United Machine Workers' Association
1880s

efforts among the non-members who were 'reaping where they have not sown'.

While the litho-printers rejoiced in their emblem, the pattern-makers, now a union of roughly similar size and funds, were rejecting for the third time in ten years pleas from their branches for an emblem. A little earlier the union leaders had been provoked into inviting members to submit a design and to send in enough orders to cover the cost. This, drily remarked William Mosses some 30 years later, was 'quite sufficient to quash the wish for an emblem until at all events we became more opulent'. It must be noted, though, that at the same time the union put £1,000 into the Clyde Trust Funded Debt at 3 per cent. and lived to regret it.

Another craft organisation, the United Machine Workers, as determined as the patternmakers to stay independent of the much larger and growing engineers' union, must have found an emblem, no matter how costly, a useful aid to competition. In their emblem the architectural plinth laid down by convention is used to indicate which workers the union regarded as its province. Indeed, the whole, a competent Blades, East and Blades job, has something of the air of a catalogue despite the classic figure with sword, scale and horn of plenty, the dove of peace and the motto borrowed from the ASE emblem (page 22). The machine workers' union, founded in 1844, merged with the ASE after the First World War and the emblem is one of the few traces of their long history, for today's engineering union holds no records for them.

Survival with independence, when working parallel to the giant craft unions, was easier for those societies based on Scotland, which more often found it possible to preserve both freedom of action and friendly relations with the English union, coupled sometimes with a higher degree of militancy. The bitter in-fighting between the Amalgamated Carpenters and the General Union did not affect the Associated Carpenters of Scotland. They kept a special brand of militancy and abstinence from 'politics' (declining for this reason to affiliate to trades councils), though they joined in the fight to repeal the Master and Servant Act which weighed especially hard on Scots workers.

Formed in 1861, the Associated Carpenters and Joiners tried to follow their English brothers in registering as a Friendly Society. But the all-seeing eye of the Registrar spotted an 'objectionable matter' in their rules which appeared to sanction strikes. So the Scots, reports Higenbottam in his history of the Woodworkers, decided not to register, nor did they bother even after the 1871 Act. They paraded their intention to work for 'the advancement of trade interests' on their emblem (page 41). In the late 1880s, the Scots union was advancing into England and by 1911, when it was taking steps to merge with the English union, it had two dozen branches south of the border. Perhaps this is why Scotland is dropped from the title, although the Lion remains discreetly panelled below St Joseph, the No. 1 Society member.

Likewise independent, militant, and friendly with the brother English organisation was the Associated Ironmoulders of Scotland, founded as the Scottish Ironmoulders' Union in 1831, after a false start in 1829. They supported Doherty's National Association for the Protection of Labour at the start, perhaps because, as Fyrth and Collins report in their history of the foundry-workers, the Scots founders were helped by a friendly cotton spinner in setting up their union. Like all craft workers deeply concerned in controlling the number of craftsmen competing for steady work, they tried all the prescribed remedies—tramping, taking shares in a co-operative foundry and helping hundreds to emigrate.

In the 'eighties emigration was reaching tidal-wave proportions. The emblem shows much less of the craft spirit than the main English foundry workers' emblem (page 23) but this is perhaps a sign of changing fashions, for in the 1830s the first emblem of the Scots is identical with that of the English, with the exception of the Scots' motto 'United to protect both master and man', a sentiment likely to appeal to the signatory James Jack. Jack, leader of the Scots founders from 1879 to 1911, was strong on capital-labour collaboration. One traditional element in the emblem is the head of Tubal Cain, who, as all bible students will know, was the first worker in metal. The emphasis here, though,

Associated Carpenters and Joiners
Alexander Gow, 1880s

in this emblem designed and printed by Johnstone of Edinburgh (now merged with Morrison and Gibb) is on industry, for the trade was going through far-reaching technological change, accelerating the rank-and-file demand for all foundry workers to be in one union. The Scots and English, thanks mainly to difficult conditions imposed by the 1876 Amalgamation Act, took until 1918 to merge fully.

To have all workers in one industry in the same union was the avowed aim of the Amalgamated Society of Railway Servants, which had started life with a bang in 1872, winning 17,000 members, and then going into the doldrums for more than a decade until the plodding Edwin Harford took over the leadership in 1884. His predecessor, Evans, had left the job under a cloud, as Harford was to do 13 years later, having painstakingly built the union to nearly 30,000 members.

It was a tough job, organising men whose status in the eyes of management is reflected in the title of the society. The General Manager of the London North Western Railway declared 'you might as well have an amalgamated society in the army'. Conditions were appalling: excessive hours (in one notorious accident case a man was on duty for 40 hours), high accident risk (in 1887 shunters and brakemen had a 1 in 20 chance of injury), and lack of compensation (ASRS records for that year show a seven-page list of orphans receiving weekly payments from the union).

Aggressive action was needed rather than the old Friendly Society approach, which also by high contributions tended to discourage recruiting. The static approach is reflected in the emblem (page 44), and it was frustration with Harford's leadership that led to the forming of the short-lived General Railway Workers' Union in 1889, which declared it would remain a fighting organisation and not be 'encumbered' with any sick fund.

Drive and aggressiveness at this period brought in 65,000 members in one year to the Amalgamated Sailors' and Firemen's Union, started with 15 men in Sunderland during 1887 by Havelock Wilson—a larger-than-life story told by Wilson in his *My Stormy Voyage Through Life*. Aggressiveness was needed to

Associated Ironmoulders of Scotland
Johnstones of Edinburgh, 1880s

Amalgamated Society of Railway Servants
1888

National Amalgamated Sailors' and Firemens' Union
Tutill & Fowiniss, 1891

organise masses of workers that the more conventional union leaders thought unorganisable. Wilson was hated by the ship-owners, themselves an aggressive lot, and complacently records that his face appeared on dozens of banners at miners' galas and union rallies in the North-East.

Havelock Wilson's face with its dapper moustache appears on the shoulders of the fireman in the emblem (page 45), which dates from November 1891, while Samuel Plimsoll, veteran advocate for the seamen's cause, appears in the guise of a bearded sailor. The emblem is a mixture of the old and the new, and the colours selected are pale, something which was to become more common in the emblems of the late 'nineties. The name of Geo. Tutill, artist, appears at the foot of the emblem, perhaps the one who exhibited 'Scarborough Castle' at the Royal Academy in the 1840s, though that would have made him an old man when this work was done. In fact it is only nominally his work: he registered it at Stationers Hall, whose record shows the 'author' to be William Fowiniss of the Finsbury Technical College.

At one point in his efforts to organise the seamen, Wilson came up against Captain Leman of the defunct Amalgamated Society for the Protection of Seamen. Leman turned out to be an agent of the Trade Protectionists, or 'sugar bounty' men (the sugar political lobby has a long history), which was trying to use the Labour movement as a political lever against the Liberals.

Back in 1872, Patrick Kenney (with the help of the carpenters' leader Robert Applegarth) had begun to organise some of the 250,000 builders' labourers into the General Labourers' Amalgamated Union. As the emblem shows, he followed general craft notions in his organisation, taking strong control over local branches and causing several of them to withdraw and start their own labourers' union.

The GLAU affiliated to the TUC, but in the meantime Kenney had been taken under the wing of the sugar bounty men, and as a result was involved in a near brawl at the 1881 London TUC with the Secretary of the TUC Political Committee, Henry Broad-hurst, a mason and old craft-style leader, very much a liberal and

General Labourers' Amalgamated Union 1880s

AMALGAMATED
ASSOCIATION OF
CARD & BLOWING
ROOM OPERATIVES

ESTD 1886

HONEST
LABOUR
BEARS A
LOVELY
FACE

LABOUR
SHALL
REFRESH
ITSELF
WITH HOPE

This is to Certify

that _____ was admitted a Member of _____
District of this Amalgamated Society on the _____
day of _____ 18 _____

_____ District Secretary   Wm Mullin General Secretary

at one time in the Home Office under Gladstone. Five TUC delegates were excluded because it was discovered that the sugar bounty men had paid their expenses. Kenney was not excluded, but, with Kelly, swore vengeance on Broadhurst. Charges and counter-charges followed, until in 1888 at a dinner following an international Trades Union Congress Kenney was found with restaurant spoons in his pocket and got 15 months' hard labour. There is, according to Raymond Postgate's history of the builders, evidence that the spoons were planted.

Kenney went to jail, Kelly became a leader of a strike-breaking organisation, but the GLAU survived with 59 other building labourers' unions founded in the 1890s, which eventually died out or were absorbed in the post-1918 amalgamations.

The 'eighties, too, saw women beginning to arrive in larger numbers in the trade-union movement, largely unnoticed at first, but soon to make their presence powerfully felt. They had long made up a large proportion of the workers in the cotton industry, particularly in the cardroom where material was prepared for the spinners. Earlier attempts at cardroom organisation tended to ignore or exclude the women, but once the Amalgamated Association of Card and Blowing Room Operatives was launched in 1885 and began to recruit the women, they swiftly showed their spirit.

In his study of the cotton unions H. A. Turner reports that the cardroom organisers handled hundreds of disputes for the women in a few years, and by the early twentieth century they accounted for a large share of the total number of women trade unionists.

Except for the poetic quotations there is little here to show that the emblem represents a union. The chief interest lies in the detailed picture of textile processes and machinery. The same could be said of other textile-union emblems like those of the hosiery workers, loom overlookers and dyers, which are the work of one man who is to figure largely in this story from now on.

This is Alexander Gow, possibly from the firm of Gow, Butterfield which produced the spinners' emblem and later coloured versions of the foundryworkers' and masons' emblems in the 1880s. By this time Gow seems to have set up on his own and was

Amalgamated Association of Card and Blowing Room Operatives
Alexander Gow, 1890

doing substantial business in the union movement. His work makes great use of photo-lithography and also, as we shall see, of scissors and paste. The lady with the distaff in the cardroom emblem is twin sister to the lady in the 1892 emblem of the newly-launched Amalgamated Tin-Plate Workers (page 17).

Since the new union could not use as a centrepiece the old gild coat of arms which the established General Tin-Plate Workers had used (see page 15), Gow obligingly filled the space with a suitable adaptation from the cardroom emblem. The Amalgamated Society of Dyers, based mainly on the Yorkshire woollen trade, is a difficult union to pin down, partly because trade unionists in each cotton and woollen town would at one time or another set up an 'amalgamation' in an attempt to draw together different districts. Most of them never reached the full national unity they sought, though there were dyers' amalgamations in Bolton, Huddersfield and Bradford between 1850 and 1890.

The Society whose emblem we still have seems to be the one set up in Bradford in 1871, and collapsed, to be reformed in 1878. Some sources say this was confined to Bradford, but Ben Turner, whose General Union of Textile Workers eventually merged in 1936 with the Amalgamated Dyers, believes that this society grew slowly after the great Bradford lockout of 1890-91, when mill-owner Sam Lister, with yearly profits of £138,000, forced wage-cuts amounting to £7,000 on 1,100 of his workers. There were pitched battles with the police and blacklegs were brought in, for whom the strikers issued a funeral card to those 'who departed from all respect, December 31, 1890'.

The dyers' leaders must have been more adventurous than those of Ben Turner's union, for he says 'Well do I remember the times when we tried to get the union to get a banner for demonstrations and an emblem for the members. I think the union executive were afraid to spend money to launch out to do something for fear of the members complaining and criticising at the half yearly meeting'. The emblem, said Turner, is the union's 'spice advertisement'. And that was what it proved to be in the great competition of the 'nineties between the 'old' and 'new' unions.

Amalgamated Society of Dyers
Alexander Gow, 1892

UNITED WE STAND. DIVIDED WE FALL.

AMALGAMATED SOCIETY OF DYERS, &c.

ESTABLISHED 1878.

WE DYE TO LIVE.

This is to Certify that
was admitted a Member of the above Society
on the   day of   18
                                          President
                              General Secretary

'I pledge you my word that if you stand firm and don't waver, within six months we will claim and win the eight-hour day'.

No more audacious pledge was ever made in the trade-union movement than that given by Will Thorne to the London gas-workers as they marched to Canning Town Hall on 31 March 1889. Consider: these men were on a 12-hour day, working 24 hours on some shifts. Thorne did not even have a union. A gas-worker from the Midlands, who could not even read or write, his first attempt to form a union at Beckton, where the workers received savage jail sentences for 'conspiracy' in 1872, had failed.

Thorne's 'pledge' was in fact a union recruiting speech, and 800 men took him at his word. The new union, the Gasworkers and General Labourers, won the eight-hour day first in London then throughout the country, in five months, not six, and by the autumn was nearly 20,000 strong. It was soon organising with equal audacity workers in other industries and the gasworkers had their emblem designed and printed by Alexander Gow (page 54). While not in the class of Blades, East and Blades work, Gow's emblem shows the fighting spirit of the new unionist, with the dominating eight-hour day slogan and clock image, challenging not only employers but old-style union leadership. Thorne, audacious or not, could not have fulfilled that pledge on his own, though as an unskilled, self-taught labourer he was an ideal leader for hundreds of thousands of men like himself outside the union movement. He had the backing of exceptional craft workers like engineers Tom Mann and John Burns, and Marxist agitators like Marx's daughter Eleanor. For them the spur was not to 'defend our rights' but to change society. This was politics rather than trade matters with a vengeance.

In its history the municipal workers' union—the gas workers' successor—recalls that 'the real business of the unions as the founders of this organisation saw it, was to fight for better wages and working conditions until the working people gained control of the state which would then do the rest'. The difference between 'old and new' ranged much wider than the issue of friendly benefits versus 'fighting contribution'.

Frederick Engels said that the new unionists differed from the 'fossilised brothers of the old trade unions', and that instead of 'craft exclusiveness', they made a 'general cry for the organisation of all trade unionists in one fraternity and for a direct struggle against capital'. This private point of view must have been shared and expressed publicly in this form, for at the time one of the ironfounders' leaders replied that though they might be termed 'fossils' they were not in the habit of 'striking one day and going round with the hat the next'.

Among the 'new' were men like A. T. Dipper, whose Tyneside labourers' union had blossomed into the National Amalgamated Union of Labour in 1889 (page 55), moving in on steel, chemical and other industries as well as shipyards, along with the gasworkers and the newly-formed dockers' union. 'That dockers and gasworkers in public utility undertakings should be competing with cranemen and similar occupations in iron- and steel-works is an indication of the lack of orderly trade unionism', is how the steelworkers' leader Sir Arthur Pugh put it some 60 years later.

It must be noted too, that half a century later Will Thorne of the gasworkers said 'My view generally has been for a fighting contribution only, but I have been compelled to change my mind'. Indeed out of the antagonism of old- and new-style trade unionism came a merging of ideas, and later of actual organisations in some cases, in an attempt to embody the virtues of both in a situation changing so fast both technologically and politically that neither could survive on one approach alone. But at that moment in time the antagonism was real and the eruption of the fighting general unions into the industrial world was both necessary and inevitable.

In the summer of 1889 the London dockers followed the gasworkers' example. A few years before, Ben Tillett, roving seaman, had come to rest in the London docks and organised a tea porters' union. He recalled in 1938 how dockers in the 1880s 'lived in doss houses at 2d, 3d and 4d a night. In the summer they slept out in the open, collecting waste rice thrown off P & O boats by the coolies'. The half-starved men who struck in the summer of

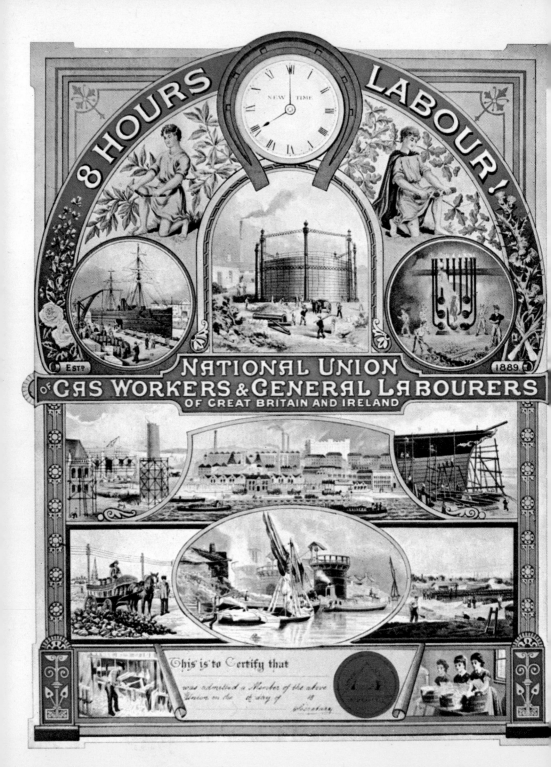

*(left) National Union of Gasworkers
and General Labourers*
Alexander Gow, 1890

*(above) National Amalgamated
Union of Labour* 1890s

1889 had no funds and were kept going by vast contributions from an aroused and sympathetic trade-union movement, including a massive contribution of £30,000 from Australian trade unionists—a return with interest for trade-union money spent in emigration grants.

Australian solidarity is celebrated in the dockers' handsome emblem by Blades, East and Blades. The copy reproduced here was sent to the Secretary of the Trades Union Congress Political Committee, Charles Fenwick, signed 'with compliments' by Tom Mann and Ben Tillett. There is a touch of irony here. By 1890 the new union wave had reached the TUC with 70,000 gasworkers and 40,000 NAUL members as well as thousands of dockers, affiliated. At the 1890 Liverpool TUC old and new clashed over the miners' demand for a legally controlled eight-hour day.

Those opposed took the general line that the eight-hour day was a trade question and not to be laid down by law. But the vote was carried, Henry Broadhurst resigned and Charles Fenwick took over as Secretary of the Political Committee. Perhaps Tom Mann intended to encourage Fenwick to do his duty, not only in the trade-union movement but also in Parliament, where he was an MP on the Liberal ticket, and where the eight-hour day bill was wending its weary way through procedure.

Such illusions on Tom Mann's part are unlikely, but if they did exist, they soon were to vanish, for Fenwick, though a miner himself, came from Northumberland where, as in Durham, the miners in certain special circumstances worked a seven-hour day which they feared to lose, and they believed the legal eight-hour day would kill this special position. Fenwick opposed the eight-hour day both at the TUC and in Parliament, provoking the newly-formed Miners' Federation of Great Britain into votes of censure and finally into uniting with the 'new' unions to throw Fenwick out of the TUC leadership.

The Miners' Federation, formed in 1889 and including about half of the country's 600,000 miners, was, apart from the general unions, one of the biggest single forces in the trade-union movement. It was headed by men of stature like Sam Pickard, iron-

Dock, Wharf, Riverside and General Labourers' Union 1891

MIDLAND MINERS' FEDERATION

STAFFORD

WARWICK

COUNCILLOR E. EDWARDS

SHROPSHIRE

WORCESTER

SISTER DORA WALSALL.

STAFFORDSHIRE

CANNOCK & RUGELY.

THIS IS TO CERTIFY THAT
was admitted a Member of The Midland Miners'
Association on the day of

Enoch Edwards President
B. Dean Treasurer
Albert Stanley Secretary

UNITED WE STAND.

DIVIDED WE FALL.

hard Sabbatarian leader of the Yorkshire miners (united a decade before), and Enoch Edwards, of the more recently formed Midlands Miners' Federation (1885-86).

The Midland Miners' emblem, produced by Alexander Gow probably in 1893, is one of the best examples of what marked the miners' organisations—regional pride and solidarity, strong figures in the leadership, and an intense interest in using political influence to change coalfield conditions. Miners' emblems always celebrate the persons of their leaders, who were not just officials but, in the villages where most miners lived, community leaders. They needed tough personalities to face up to the pit owners, who like the steelmasters thought nothing of evicting families in winter during strikes. When working-class JPs began to be appointed, School Boards elected and the new county councils formed, and with the extension of rural franchise, the miners responded. Leaders' portraits are suitably labelled with the new titles of Councillor, JP or MP. Like the Yorkshire, Derbyshire and later Durham emblems, the Midlands' emblem reflects pride in the solid miners' headquarters buildings of the time, regional history in coats of arms, places of interest and incidents which touched miners closely.

Sister Dora of Walsall, shown in an emblem panel tending the injured at the 1875 Birchills Ironworks explosion, is a local heroine with a statue in Walsall, and the emblem panel is from the same source as one of the scenes engraved on the memorial. A remarkable woman, Dorothy Patterson was the daughter of a Yorkshire rector who refused to let her follow Florence Nightingale to the Crimea; she received her nursing training with an order of nuns, and ran their small hospital in Walsall, was nurse to local railway workers and fought smallpox epidemics.

She was at the pithead in the Pelsall Mining disaster in 1872, when 22 died and, when the Birchills furnace exploded killing 11 men, Sister Dora with two others, according to the account supplied me by the Walsall librarian, tended the dying when 'not even the doctors could stand the stench, agony and horror of nursing them'.

Midland Miners' Federation
Alexander Gow, 1893

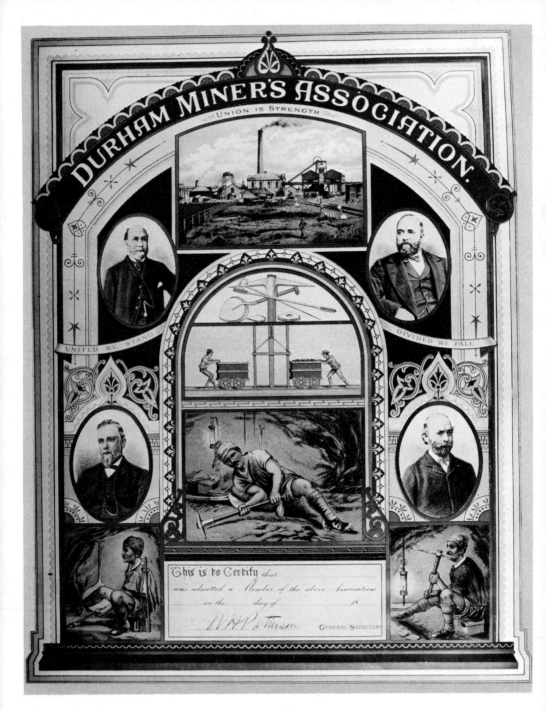

Durham Miners' Association
Alexander Gow, 1890s

Mock-up for the Emblem of Ashton (Lancs) Miners
Alexander Gow, 1893

With first Burt (Northumberland) and MacDonald (Scotland) and later Fenwick (Northumberland) and Crawford (Durham) in Parliament, the miners should have been strongly placed to press their demand for a legal eight-hour day. But the MPs, from the point of view of the miners' federation, were mainly from the wrong places. Though the TUC passed resolutions each year, Fenwick for example, stuck to his own opinion 'and that of his constituents'.

As Page Arnot records in his saga of the miners from 1889-1910, during the Parliamentary debate Randolph Churchill mocked Burt for his contradictory position on the eight-hour day. Page Arnot also records how the Federation leaders in their campaign for the eight-hour day were 'twitted' with being 'new' trade unionists. Fenwick was not shifted from his TUC position until 1894 when the votes of the miners, general unions and others replaced him with Woods, a miners' nominee.

The Durham Miners' emblem (page 60), designed by Gow in the early 'nineties, still carries the portrait of the miners' leader and MP William Crawford, though he had died in 1890. This emblem was used until 1900, when Gow designed another carrying pictures of county scenes, retired miners' homes and the portraits of new leaders, headed by the venerable J. H. Wilson MP, another stern Methodist, who stiffened the resistance to the eight-hour day. The same pressures that shifted Fenwick had removed him from the TUC political committee in 1893.

Within the miners' federation, the districts had great autonomy, and so did the 'local' unions within the districts. The Ashton, Haydock and Bolton Miners' Union was a 'local' union dating from 1882, though the term is misleading. At its peak in 1893, the Ashton union had 12,000 members, about one-third of the organised miners in Lancashire and Cheshire, so it is not surprising it should decide on an emblem. What is shown on page 61 is in fact a mock-up for an emblem composed on the basis of the Durham Miners' emblem with the Ashton title pasted over and the portraits of the Durham leaders cut out, while photographs of the Ashton leaders have been taped in at the back. The whole operation was done, probably in the Wigan offices, using gummed receipts borrowed from Edwin Walkden, the secretary.

For some reason, whoever did this—perhaps the ubiquitous Alexander Gow himself—baulked at transferring the whole of the Durham centre-piece. Instead he cut it out and pasted in the picture of the slaves with the fabulous bundle of sticks, taken from the gasworkers' emblem (page 54). Since Gow designed all three emblems, he was presumably entitled to do so, but this type of emblem, done at high speed with much borrowed material, was tending to reduce standards.

In some cases Gow seems to have cut costs, but generally he seems to have operated around the 2s 6d charged by other firms, though what he was producing was becoming more and more stereotyped as he took on more and more business in the emblem boom. This was stimulated by the competition between established unions and new unions as the general unions moved into other industries.

One group of workers who received the attention of the new unions after previous years of neglect were the enginemen, cranemen, boilermen and firemen. The TUC resolution of 1888 calling for a Steam Engine and Boiler bill to 'secure competent men and minimise the danger to which workers are subject by cheap and inexperienced labour' has a touch of the more narrow craft arrogance. But at this time the enginemen were beginning to organise at pithead, in steel mill, gas-works and shipyard, and ten years later four separate enginemen's unions were affiliated to the TUC. Which union has left its trace in the emblem on page 64 must remain a matter of guesswork. Two of the four died out, one merged later with the steelworkers and one survived, linked to both miners and transport workers, until finally absorbed recently into the TGWU.

One enginemen's union was represented at the TUC by John Baker. He, according to Sir Arthur Pugh in his book *Men of Steel*, led his union to a merger with the steelworkers in 1911. An organiser of the old school, Baker spiced his bulletins with passages quoted from Carlyle and John Stuart Mill, a habit that

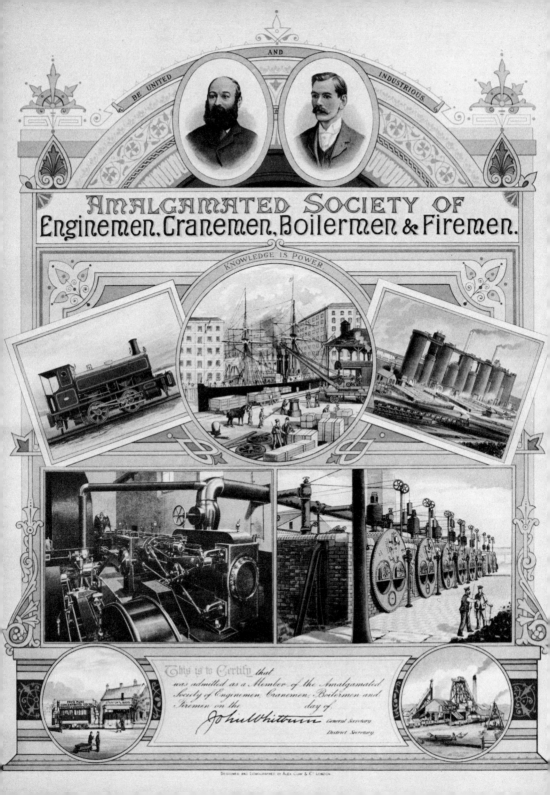

BE UNITED · AND · INDUSTRIOUS

AMALGAMATED SOCIETY OF
Enginemen, Cranemen, Boilermen & Firemen.

KNOWLEDGE IS POWER

This is to Certify that
was admitted as a Member of the Amalgamated
Society of Enginemen, Cranemen, Boilermen and
Firemen on the   day of

John Whitburn General Secretary

District Secretary

DESIGNED AND LITHOGRAPHED BY ALEX. LOW & Co. LONDON.

dies hard. (About ten years ago at a car factory strike meeting, a worker appealed for a return to work, clinching his argument with a quotation from Carlyle. Another striker, who won by a large majority, riposted with a quotation from Tom Mann).

This leaves us with the other union whose TUC delegate was a Councillor Copley, and here again Sir Arthur Pugh is helpful, for he recalls the steel smelters in 1893 rejecting an approach from district official Copley on the grounds that they had experienced trouble with his national union leader John Whitburn, the signatory of this emblem. So it looks as though this is the union that eventually joined the TGWU, and since TGWU records on the enginemen do not pre-date 1900, this emblem by Gow would seem to be the only evidence from that period.

At least half the surviving emblems from this period are the work of Alexander Gow, and the fitful traces he left have proved one of the most tantalising trails pursued in the search for the background of this area of trade-union history. The records of the London Master Printers for the 1890s show no trace of him, nor, apparently, did he advertise in the *British Printer*, the *British Lithographer* or similar journals. The Lithographic Printers did not include him in their lists issued to members, nor have the Litho Artists heard of him. And the Board of Trade does not have his name on their register of business names. One expert in the field thinks Gow might have been a lithographic draughtsman working with different printers, but several emblems bear the legend 'designed and Lithographed by Alexander Gow & Co'.

One thing seems clear: Gow was in good standing with the trade-union movement, for in March 1894 the London Society of Compositors, heir to at least a century's tradition of organisation in the capital, chose him to make them a new trade emblem to match their new St Bride's headquarters (shown in the emblem, page 67) and their new rules. It sold at 2s a copy and might have been subsidised, for it is well below the 2s 9d paid by the Lithoprinters for their emblem. The compositors, who had been campaigning for several years for Fair Practices, could not have chosen an unrecognised firm for this of all jobs.

Amalgamated Society of Enginemen, etc.
Alexander Gow, 1890s

But why did they not choose the superior workmanship of Blades, East and Blades, whose chief, William Blades, had backed them in the fair practices fight? Their craft emblem, incorporating the Stationers' Guild coat of arms, would seem to have been an obvious job for that firm. Furthermore, Drummond of the compositors was an old friend of Blades, and after his death raised money to save his collection of books, which later became the nucleus of the St Bride's Printing Library. True, Drummond had resigned in 1893 because of political differences with his more radical colleagues—Drummond was a Tory. But if this led to a break in the connection with Blades, East and Blades, or if cheapness and swiftness had been the basis for the choice, nevertheless a few years later the compositors went back to the old firm to have their jubilee souvenir printed.

At the same time the Patternmakers, slowly making up their minds, asked Blades, East and Blades to produce an emblem (page 68). William Mosses recalls that 'the rough outline was furnished by an eminent artist Mr Walter Crane, whilst one of our Woolwich members with exceptional artistic gifts completed the actual design.' How far Crane went with his work and why he did not complete the design is not recorded. Crane, a friend and co-worker with William Morris, designed the Electrical Trades Union banner and much other work associated with the Labour movement. But perhaps trade-union emblems were not to his liking. The need to assemble a variety of obligatory elements and relate them in a pattern dictated not entirely by artistic considerations, but by the reconciling of various opinions and interests within the client organisation, may have presented a task that did not appeal to him.

Earlier in the century, craft tradition provided conventions for the ordering of elements within the emblem and artists were in any case often schooled in the eighteenth-century trade sign and near-heraldic type of work demanded. Later there were no such commonly accepted rules. The artist either worked to the client's order, or the client accepted *in toto* the artist's interpretation (though this must have been rare). Sometimes the artist, as often

London Society of Compositors
Alexander Gow, 1894

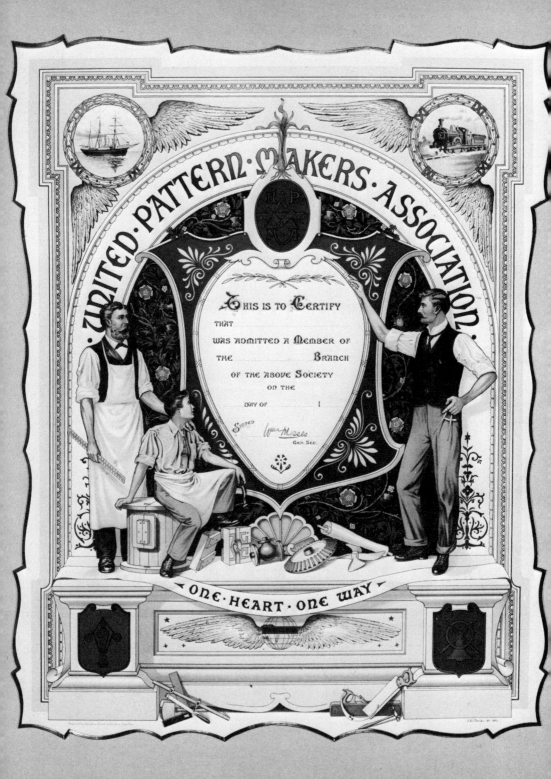

happened with late nineteenth-century commercial lithography, was virtually excluded. Or perhaps Gow's scissors-and-paste methods and the photo-transfer process got to work.

A last tantalising clue about Gow's identity comes from Sir Arthur Pugh in his account of the British Steel Smelters' emblem, (page 71) decided on in April 1892, after a visit to the executive meeting of the Association by Mr Gow, 'representative of a firm producing emblems, banners and such like regalia'. The emblem carries the imprint *Alex. Gow and Co., Litho, London*.

'There were few active members of the union who did not adorn his home with an emblem certifying the date of his entry into the union, signed by the general secretary, mounted in a suitable frame', writes Pugh. And emblems continued to adorn parlour and club-room walls until well into the twentieth century. Only a few months ago a framed copy of the Amalgamated Society of Railway Servants emblem was taken down from the wall by a branch about to merge with another and handed to the head office of the National Union of Railwaymen.

But few new emblems were produced after 1900. The Spinners and the Typographical Association had new designs in 1907 and the Amalgamated Society of Engineers' emblem was in use up to the 1914-18 war. With the great wave of amalgamations after the First World War the style and title of many old unions disappeared and the new unions were too big for emblem issues, preferring the more popular badges. For a while the Amalgamated Society of Woodworkers over-printed the old Carpenters' emblem, but as a general rule their use was as awards to long-service members.

In any case successive insurance acts changed the emphasis on the friendly benefit side which had been so important in nineteenth-century union life and made the emblem something to be carefully preserved. And there were more subtle changes of fashion. In 1937 the Iron and Steel Trades Confederation decided to award a shield with the confederation crest to branch officers and others for meritorious service 'introducing a distinctive note which is so often lacking in the old type of emblem'.

United Patternmakers' Association
G. Twist and W. Crane, 1897

The boilermakers kept their emblem design embodied in badge and letterheading until 1959, their 125th anniversary, when they discarded the design with its obsolete machinery and happily also the 'God helps those' motto with its obsolete morality, returning to the motto chosen originally by William Hughes in 1834—'Humani Nihil Alienum'.

Today emblems are collectors' pieces, especially the engravings of the period 1820-60. Many unions do not know that such things exist in their past. Grappling with the problems of the present in a changing world when current documentation demands space at the expense of earlier material, they may well find history a luxury. All the more reason to hope that the splendid idea of a central institute-museum of the Labour movement will find the support it deserves, for surely emblems like these, now preserved in the Trades Union Congress Library, will there find appropriate recognition. As one trade union official has said: 'We really have no space for such things. We have to think of today. But once in a while it does us good to get them out, look at them, and refresh the spirit a bit'.

British Steel Smelters' Amalgamated Association
Alexander Gow, 1893

BOOKS REFERRED TO IN THE TEXT

Page Arnot, R. *The Miners: History of the Miners' Federation of Great Britain* London 1949

Chandler, F. *History of the Almalgamated Society of Carpenters and Joiners* London 1910

Cummings, D. C. *Historical Survey of the Boilermakers Society* Newcastle 1905

Fyrth, H. J. and Collins H. *The Foundryworkers* Manchester 1959

Gosden, P. H. J. H. *The Friendly Societies in England 1815–1875* Manchester 1961

Higenbottam, S. *Our Society's History* London 1939

Jefferys, B. *The Story of the Engineers* London 1946

Kidd, A. T. *History of the Tinplate Workers* London 1949

Kiddier, W. *The Old Trade Unions* London 1930

Mosses, William *History of the Patternmakers 1872–1922* London 1922

Musson, A. E. *The Congress of 1868* TUC, London 1968

Pennell, J. and E. R. *Lithography and Lithographers* London 1915

Postgate, R. *The Builders' History* London 1923

Pugh, A. *Men of Steel* London 1951

Smiles, Samuel *Self Help* Centenary Edition, London 1958

Turner, Ben *Short History of the General Union of Textile Workers* Heckmondwike 1920

Turner, H. A. *Trade Union Growth and Structure: A Comparative Study of the Cotton Unions* London 1962

Webb, Sidney and Beatrice *The History of Trade Unionism* Longmans, London 1911

ACKNOWLEDGEMENTS

The publisher and author wish to thank the following for their co-operation and assistance in the reproduction of emblems:

The TUC librarian, Mr E. E. Brown; the National Union of Sheet Metal Workers; Oddfellows Manchester Unity; the Amalgamated Society of Boilermakers, Shipwrights, Blacksmiths and Structural Workers; the National Society of Brushmakers; the Amalgamated Union of Engineering and Foundryworkers (Foundry Section).

Thanks for help in obtaining information about these emblems is also due, in particular, to the officials of the National Graphical Association, the Amalgamated Union of Building Trade Workers, the National Union of Railwaymen, the Amalgamated Association of Operative Cotton Spinners and Twiners, the Association of Patternmakers and Allied Craftsmen, the Transport and General Workers' Union, and to the librarians of the Trades Union Congress, the St Bride's Printing Library, the Marx Memorial Library and the Libraries of the Borough of Walsall.

The author's personal thanks go especially to Mr Edmund Frow, who gave many valuable clues, and to Mr James Klugmann, Mr Ted Brake, Mr Ray Watkinson, Mr Frank Jackson, Mr George Lagrue and Mr Harry Watson for their help and advice.